Living with Shadows

Eric R Fraser

Order this book online at www.trafford.com
or email orders@trafford.com

Most Trafford titles are also available at major online book retailers.

© Copyright 2011 Eric R Fraser.
All rights reserved. No part of this publication may be reproduced, stored in a retrieval system, or transmitted, in any form or by any means, electronic, mechanical, photocopying, recording, or otherwise, without the written prior permission of the author.

The views expressed in this work are solely those of the author and do not necessarily reflect the views of the publisher, and the publisher hereby disclaims any responsibility for them.

Print information available on the last page.

ISBN: 978-1-4269-3764-4 (sc)
ISBN: 978-1-4269-3765-1 (e)

Library of Congress Control Number: 2011912438

Trafford rev. 04/08/2015

 www.trafford.com

North America & international
toll-free: 1 888 232 4444 (USA & Canada)
fax: 812 355 4082

My story is about living with schizophrenia and begins with an interview by an undergraduate nurse on March 17, 2005.

Interviewer: So, I'm going to just start asking questions and I will redirect you as you kind of get off track. I'll ask you some more information. I might write a little bit. Don't stop talking just ignore me. So just keep telling me whatever comes to mind. Don't think too much. Tell me who you are Eric?

Eric: Okay. I'm a Business Administration graduate from Red River College. Let's see. I came from out of town. I was born in Swan Lake hospital. I think it's close to Mariapolis and that's where I first lived. Then we moved to Glenboro. We lived there for 8 years or so. After that we came to Winnipeg and have lived here since 1988.

Interviewer: So you went to high school here, or?

Eric: I went to nursery school and elementary school in Glenboro and then when we came here I went to French immersion from Grade 4 up to Grade 6. Three years. And then I went to an English school, because the French immersion was too difficult for me with my auditory processing it was hard for me to keep up with the schoolwork. I needed a tutor. Why I didn't get one I don't know.

Interviewer: Did the school identify that you were having difficulty at that time?

Eric: Yes. It wasn't until Grade 6 and by that time it was too late. They tried helping, but it wasn't working and then finally I went to an English speaking school in grade 7. It was Minnetonka and I had a counselor there who helped me plan and organize my homework. Compared to the French immersion school I hardly received any homework at the English school. It seemed easier. I was happier and I was a lot less stressed.

Interviewer: Did you like school?

Eric: No. I detested school. But I liked college. College is fun because you can do whatever you want. You are learning on your own. You can learn what you want to learn.

Interviewer: So would they identify that you were having some difficulty learning at that point or being organized?

Eric: Learning and being organized, but the French immersion school really didn't have anything in place to help me, like tutors or anything like that. I don't know if it was because of the funding or they just figured I could do it on my own. I had poor time management skills back then. If I hated to do something, I procrastinated the homework to the bitter end. I even got extensions. But after the extension I would only get a few marks off and then I would actually get a good grade. [At that time, my learning disability had just been identified with actual measurable guidelines. (1986). It was my second grade teacher teaching for her very first year that was able to identify or suggest what my learning disability could be.]

Interviewer: So did you hang around with friends?

Eric: A few friends and then after high school, a friend of mine from junior high wanted to carpool to college. We did for the first three months and then we just parted ways. I guess he left because he thought it was too hard, but I really don't know. But because I was used to the French immersion school and the private high school as both gave me a lot of homework I was fairly used to it. At college I found out the hard way that I could only handle four courses at a time. I wish I would have went to a counsellor sooner to get help for my learning disability and get funding for tutors and whatever for schooling. Then I wouldn't have been as stressed, and then I probably would have had a less traumatic experience with my psychosis or I may have even avoided it, but who knows.

Interviewer: Do you think that the stress may have caused the psychosis?

Eric: Part of it. Yes. But it could have been the alcohol I consumed and I knew some people, who smoked pot, but I didn't smoke it, but I could smell it second-hand. I believe that didn't help at all.

Interviewer: So tell me when was it the first time you knew that something wasn't quite right?

Eric: When I started feeling highs and lows and then I would feel too many emotions in a matter of milliseconds. I would feel free and then the next minute I felt imprisoned. But when I decided that something was wrong I couldn't even speak, I couldn't think, I just couldn't do anything. I was crippled.

Interviewer: How old were you then?

Eric: I had just turned 20.

Interviewer: So you were already at college?

Eric: Yes. It was my second year, but I was only half way through my course at Red River College. So from January to February 1999 while I was there my psychosis started to be more aggressive. Even though I was taking five courses at that time. Later something scared me so I decided to quit and the college asked me why. Well they didn't ask me but I wrote on a paper as to why and I put down personal because I didn't know what the problem was. I basically thought well I quit so I went home and sat around.

Interviewer: What did your parents say about it?

Eric: I think they were shocked. They thought and said, "No, you didn't quit." Go back to school. You really didn't quit. I thought I had because I wrote on a piece of paper that I did. I went back a few times and one of those times I saw a counsellor there and he had a disability. He was a paraplegic. His name was Tim Thurston and I talked to him and I said I want to go back to being a kid. I was thinking really hard and I wanted to escape in my mind, away from the reality and he said to me, "Do you know how to get into the hospital?" I can't remember what I said but I said I was pretty sure, but he said, "I'll tell you anyway." So he said basically go to the emergency, see a doctor and then they'll take you through. Like he described it! Go through a tunnel all the way. He didn't say McEwen. He just said you'll go to a bed or a room and they'll take you there and they'll look after you. And that's exactly what happened.

Interviewer: So what did you do? You came home and said Mom, Dad, I have to go to the hospital.

Eric: I was on the stairs, at the top of the stairs, and I basically said, or I didn't say, I was writing a bunch of stuff down as well, because I couldn't think, I couldn't speak, so I was writing out thoughts and one particular thought kept running through my head, but I …… my Mom asked me and said, "Do you want to go the hospital?" because my Mom had talked to the counsellor and I said, "Yes." Or I nodded yes and my parents said, "We have to go now." "Let's go now." We went to the hospital and saw the doctor, the doctor talked to my parents and my sister.

Interviewer: Your sister is younger or older?

Eric: Younger. And basically I guess the doctor was telling them that I had to go to McEwen because there was some kind of mental illness occurring. Because physically he could tell there was nothing wrong, because they took my blood pressure and checke my reflexes and things like that.

Interviewer: How did you feel about going and staying there?

Eric: Well, I was like, "Good something is going to be done. It wasn't until I got to the bedroom that I felt relieved that I was there. I was away from college and all the stress. All the worries were gone, temporarily! But the minute they tried taking my ID away, I said, "No. I want to keep it. Otherwise, I felt my identity was going to be erased or rewritten like everything else was. I don't know what it is. It's when you're sick you just want to hang on to things you remember and you want to hang on to things that you know at that time are connecting you to something like your past.

Interviewer: Did they take anything else from you?

Eric: They took anything that I could use to kill myself with, just in case.

Interviewer: Were you having thoughts like that?

Eric: It wasn't until later. Not until the middle and towards the end when I started feeling depressed.

Interviewer: So you are there. You are kind of feeling relieved until they start to take your identity from you, for example, your wallet.

Eric: My personal little world, my identity, is all that I had left, of what I left behind.

Interviewer: So then what's going through you mind?

Eric: I knew, like the next day, I knew that I had to get out of there somehow.

Interviewer: Keep on.

Eric: Well, maybe not the next day, but a couple of days later I knew I had to get out of there because I saw the people there and it was kind of like hopelessness. Because some of them I could figure out that they were homeless and some I could figure out that things weren't going anywhere. And it wasn't good to stay with those people because it was depressing.

Interviewer: How many other 20-year-olds were there?

Eric: I think there was a 25 or 26-year-old patient. There were a few older men. Some of the patients were in their 30's and some were really old. Some of the older men were on IV's and some were just content. Oh, and some of them were female patients. And I remember one of the women went into the room where it's just pure wall and one door and she went and cried in there.

Interviewer: Like a seclusion room?

Eric: Yeah. But I thought if I go crazy, like really nuts, I hope I don't get put in there. I don't want to be locked in there.

Interviewer: They never secluded you?

Eric: No. No.

Interviewer: What was helpful during that hospital stay?

Eric: The nurses were pretty good. They made sure I got my meds. They got me doing things like activities that were there, but they started me off with something small like stay on the floor. Maybe they were testing to see if I was compliant with their request. I was only on the second floor so I wasn't as bad in terms of my condition. I wasn't as bad or severe as other people. (According to the severity of a patient's illness you were put on a higher floor. Because my illness was 'mild' enough to control I was put on the second floor or ground level. In the basement they had kids or mostly teenagers.)

Interviewer: What did they tell you about your condition?

Eric: They hadn't told me anything. It wasn't until June 14, 1999 that I was diagnosed. My psychiatrist that I am with now, and good friends with, he diagnosed me, and I didn't believe him at first because I was still disillusioned or delusional or hallucinatory. A little bit, not as much as when I was first in the hospital, but I was in disbelief or denial as people call it. He said something that really scared me; he said, "You know some people are actually on 18 mg of this Risperidone, and I'm thinking I'm not going that high on this drug! Man, I can't even handle, the 8 mg I was already taking, it was so sedating I couldn't function.

Interviewer: So what happened? You were admitted to hospital. The nurses were helpful. They made sure you got your meds. So what happened?

Eric: And while I was there they called me the miracle patient because I took to the meds so quickly.

Interviewer: How long do you think you had been sick prior to receiving treatment?

Eric: I would say about a month, but it was so subtle. It wasn't just like bang I had it. It was gradual and it was just slowly creeping in.

Interviewer: So tell me about that. Did your thoughts change or did you just know that you were sick?

Eric: Yes, my thoughts changed and what I saw was scary. It didn't happen instantly it was more gradual.

Interviewer: I want to understand more about how your thoughts changed. How you slipped into being ill. How that happened. You said it was not a switch, but it was very gradual.

Eric: Like maybe a month prior to it settling in maybe there was one or a couple of factors that contributed to it that would switch it on, but would only become gradual.

Interviewer: What kind of factors do you think?

Eric: Probably smelling second hand smoke of the marijuana did not help because I kind of felt dizzy. It was like no big deal at first and then I drank, like for the first time since I turned 18 so I was still getting used to the alcohol and I think that's another factor, because that made my head spin. It made me feel really disoriented.

Interviewer: So what sorts of thoughts were you starting to have in that month leading up to the psychosis?

Eric: What was I thinking? I was starting to take things more personally, like things were directed at me and only me, and certain things were hurting my heart, you know. It was just like stabbing my heart and I wanted it to stop! For example, bad comments made about people. They were about other people but I would take that as if it's me, or sounds like me.

Interviewer: So you were hearing things that other people were saying, but you were twisting them and thought they were yours.

Eric: Yes. As if they were talking to me too, so if someone else was being hurt I was being hurt. If they were happy I was happy. It was as if I could connect with the people through emotion depending on what was being said to them. It was really weird.

It was as if someone told me a stressful story or a happy story I would listen to the stressful story it would make me feel dizzy or overwhelming to the point of feeling faint. But if it was a happy story I would still get dizzy but I would feel like I was thinking freely or be happy. Meaning that I had thoughts that would connect easily from one thought to another.

Interviewer: Did you have hallucinations?

Eric: Yes I did. Hallucinations were shadows. I don't know why they were shadows. It was kind of strange. And I also didn't like the fact that there were a lot of crows that year outside. I thought, man that is so depressing. All these crows were everywhere. And I started thinking; man is God trying to say, "We're all dying." Everything is just death. It was really bizarre. And that was in the summer of 1999, but before the depressing thoughts, I was taking whatever thought was said be it an opinion or comment or negative or positive by another person I was taking it personally in the beginning. When I quit college I checked off personal problem for quitting. A commercial came on when I got home from college that same day and it said AT&T personal plan and I was like how the heck did they know that I quit (college)? I thought everyone knew that I quit now.

Interviewer: So you were seeing connections with them?

Eric: Yes.

Interviewer: Was this scary for you? Did you know that it was odd or did you think it was normal?

Eric: I felt like I was being watched. Have you ever read that book Big Brother?

Interviewer: No, but I've heard about it.

Eric: In a book called 1984. It was like I was being watched. And then what else did I think? I thought that God was giving me codes or secrets of the future ahead of time. For example, I was thinking of a 911 for a while because I liked numbers and licence plates but I didn't know what it meant or how it related to me. For all I knew it was a number that kept going through my mind and I thought maybe it's someone's birthday. It's like getting a piece of the puzzle and you don't have the rest of the puzzle.

Interviewer: How about other people watching you like your parents for instance? What would they have said about you during that time? What would they say? Would they say, our son Eric is doing really well, or would they say our son is acting a little odd, or would they have reported to a friend perhaps?

Eric: I think they would have said, oh yeah he's still at college you know, kind of putting a false front. I don't know if they actually did. They weren't sure what was going on. They thought it was a part of me growing up...making choices for myself.

Interviewer: Did they know what was going on in your head?

Eric: No. They had no clue. My Mom could sort of figure out what was going on, but during the psychotic episode I started saying things to my parents that would really hurt them because I was having a lot of psychological warfare in my head between good and evil. I would say the truth to stab them like a knife, and then my Mom actually said what I was thinking," You're cutting me with a knife with what you are saying." I was really getting nasty with them. And I was questioning them. I was questioning their beliefs and morals.

Interviewer: You were argumentative.

Eric: Yes. I basically had similar thoughts my Uncle had. I remember my Dad told me the gist of the argument. My Dad told me that my Uncle said that everyone is wrong, everything you do is wrong. That was around 1993 when my Grandmaman Fraser was alive and we'd have Sunday supper there together and my Uncle Denys lived on the street. I can relate to what he thought because I was starting to believe it too 6 years later during my psychosis. Then I thought that if I go to the Bible I could get help from it to guide me.

So I essentially read a lot of what was in the Bible and a lot of it was very confusing. It was hard to read, but you could get the gist of certain parts that were really clear. And in a sense my psychosis was confusing, like the Bible, and when I had a clear thought you could understand everything so clearly, crystal clear, and there would be quietness in my head and it would be just be ah. But right now, even my mind is still thinking a lot, but it feels like it is stuck sometimes, they're like mini-psychosis. You're so focused that you are trying to get that task done or whatever but your brain can't filter to the right thought to complete the task.

Interviewer: You said that it wasn't long after you were admitted to hospital that you thought, "I got to get out of here, I don't think I want to stay." So how long were you there anyway?

Eric: A week later I came home to sleep at night and spend the day at the hospital, but I was officially, at the hospital a month and half. Then I was in the outpatient program living at home.

Interviewer: And how did you get to come home?

Eric: I essentially had to conform to society. I had to behave like a normal human being, which was very tough! I'll tell you! If I am not having problems thinking, I'm having problems conforming.

Interviewer: So what do they expect you to do then to conform?

Eric: Basically I had to behave how I used to they would train me I guess. I don't know how, but it is a behaviour that you learn, it's not something that you talk about, it's just something you do from observation. So essentially they had me do activities with other people like cooking or cleaning up stuff, like cleaning up the kitchen and watering plants, planting, painting ornaments or you know creating stuff using your creativity.

Interviewer: Did you find that helpful or were you doing it just to conform?

Eric: There was essentially nothing else to do, but it helped because I had to make use of my hands and my arms. I had to reconnect to my body in order to function. It's because when you are in a psychosis you are stuck in your thinking. You don't really move that much so you have to use your body. You have to connect the whole body to make it one and it's kind of like trying to learn how to drive a car again. Learning where everything goes and stuff. You know it's almost like you were paralyzed, but in the brain. That's the way I look at it.

Interviewer: I think you describe this beautifully... One of the things that you mentioned earlier is you said you had suicidal thoughts towards the middle and toward the end the time. When you were ready to go home you started having these thoughts.

Eric: Yes. And my sister and my dad and my mom would take turns looking after me during the day. They would tell me saying who was staying with me that day because I gave them signals that I was really depressed. They were worried that I would try something. I think that helped that someone was there because it relieved my stress. It relieved their stress because they were looking after me and they knew that they could stop me from committing suicide. So it was a win/win situation. (My parents were told that I was suicidal and took the risk of taking me home.)

Interviewer: Did you want to commit suicide?

Eric: I thought about it and I just, I had a stronger will to live than to commit suicide.

Interviewer: Why do you think you got depressed?

Eric: It's just a chemical in the brain where it just gets you in the negative and you can't help thinking of depressing thoughts. You just can't help it. It's like you're forced to think that way. It's like you're lacking your serotonin. I need a high here. And the medication was kind of working, but I guess I was burnt out. I had used up all that I could create. It was just it was like I was out of breath for creating big thoughts. The thoughts I had were small pants of breath. It was almost like being asthmatic with a puffer.

Interviewer: So eventually you were discharged home?

Eric: Yes.

Interviewer: And how did you feel about going home?

Eric: I was quite happy, but I couldn't drive. My doctor wouldn't let me even though I had my license on me. He thought I was incapable of driving because of my thoughts. He didn't want me to endanger the lives of others. But I wanted to drive, but I was thinking so many thoughts I couldn't concentrate long enough to drive.

Interviewer: Even though he was probably right.

Eric: Yes, he was probably right, although I disagreed. I knew he was right but I thought man I want to drive!

Interviewer: How did you get out of the hospital so quickly?

Eric: Because I had to learn how to be a normal person as opposed to another schizophrenic or another manic-depressive or whatever. I knew I had to get out of there to get away from the way they behaved to the way normal people behaved.

Interviewer: Wow! I never looked at it that way. One thing I wanted to ask you was if you were sitting down with a young man who was just being admitted to the same hospital you were what would you tell him to help his stay? Do you have any advice, you know?

Eric: Actually I gave advice to a girl. She was only 17 or 18. Her brother was diagnosed a year, maybe six months before her with schizophrenia and she got so scared that she just went on every drug she could take and hung out with the wrong people and she was scared because she saw what her brother was doing and it scared the living shit out of her! Her parents said to me, whatever you said to her, you've planted the seed within her and that will remain in her as long as she remembers. I was like wow, that's powerful! I never looked at it that way. I was essentially trying to say to her don't hang around these losers because they'll make you go on the wrong track. Not only that it will make things a lot worse. But I said it differently. I can't remember how I said it, but it was in a way that I could tell her, I'm on the meds, and I'm doing well. If you just stay on the meds you will do fine. It's not going to be easy. I said, " Stay away from the drugs. Finish high school or whatever it is. Keep doing what you want to do in order for a better future." I don't know where she is now. I think she goes in and out of MATC.

Interviewer: Manitoba Adolescent Treatment Centre. Eric, are you the same person that you were before all this happened? Have you changed or are you the same? What do you think?

Eric: Some things have changed and some of it stayed the same, but I think if I had this experience I wouldn't be where I am at today. I'd be like a normal person just saying, oh my God, another day at work, blah, blah, blah. Whereas now it's because of this all of my doors have opened up. It's just amazing what I have done. I mean I finished college and I love the tutors there. They were awesome! They helped me a lot. Of course I did the legwork, but they helped me along so it was good and I'm good at marketing. I was a B average student in marketing. A little bit of my psychosis showed up while I was in college again, but it was something

I said or thought, and it just went away. It was gone.

Interviewer: Do you recognize when the psychosis, as you would call it, starts to creep in?

Eric: It's when even normal people have paranoid thoughts and it's when you start to believe those thoughts that it will cause problems whether the thoughts are true or not. For example, if a person has a little bit of distrust or jealousy and they eavesdrop on their girlfriend or boyfriend talk about another girl or boy to their friend on the phone. Then that person can ask whom they were talking about. If their boyfriend or girlfriend says they were talking about an actor or actress in a movie then that's the end of the conversation for a normal person. Whereas, someone with an illness makes you disbelieve and distrust them and then you get into an argument and may cost you the relationship.

Interviewer: Can you tell when that's happening or is it just subtle?

Eric: I see it in my relatives and other people too. For example, they'll say on a long distance call," You weren't going to call us because you live over there so you don't care." Just saying that a family member let alone anyone shouldn't say to another family member or anyone else. Family cares about other family members. Unless if the other family member is not being reasonable or respectful or deceiving. Let's put it this way, paranoia just destroys people and it's unhealthy unless if it's going to save your life. If you're being followed and someone looks suspicious then I would run or get away and call for help. That's one of the few times paranoia can help. Or you have all the facts that make sense and then the person tells you something that doesn't make sense based on your facts. Obviously then the person is lying.

Interviewer: Can you tell whether they have schizophrenia or not.

Eric: Yes. Actually, one of my friend's girlfriends was saying things that were not normal for a person. Later I found out she was given antidepressants.

Interviewer: So how is that different from schizophrenia? Or is it?

Eric: I think all people have some form of it or a little bit of it. But it's not to the point where it is debilitating the person from daily tasks in life. It's good to have a little bit but it's also good to keep it at bay and just think normal thoughts, whatever normal is. Just act like nothing is wrong. Keep your thoughts to yourself about certain topics from other people. And usually thoughts pass through so if you ignore it, it'll go away, but if you keep focusing on it, it's going to kill you or it'll make you grow, depending on where you focus your thoughts on. Like my Dad said, " Think the right thoughts." You'll know what they are once you listen to yourself.

Interviewer: You've eluded to mention your parents and your sister a little bit. How has your relationship with your parents, for instance, changed since all of this? Or has it changed?

Eric: When I had my first episode of psychosis, I didn't trust them. They essentially had to earn my trust back. And now everything is back to normal. But there's a little bit of something I can't think of right now.... I think it's lessons I learned from my parents.

Interviewer: Teaching what?

Eric: Teaching positive stuff. Things that will help you get on with life.

Interviewer: Like get up in the morning and take a shower or do you mean like opening the door for somebody else to help him or her out?

Eric: Yes. Be kind to other people. Respect other people.

Interviewer: Do you feel that they're still teaching you those things?

Eric: Yes.

Interviewer: So, tell me what the difference is, this relationship, you know, you were saying that your thoughts are different and your parents' thoughts are normal.

Eric: Yes.

Interviewer: Tell me more.

Eric: They can function as a normal person whereas it feels like I'm thinking a whole bunch of thoughts at once and I'm trying to organize it. It is harder for me to concentrate. And I see things differently with this disease than they see with their normal perception.

Interviewer: Yes.

Eric: I have like, kind of like an extra sensory perception.

Interviewer: Ok. So you do things with a sixth sense I'll call it.

Eric: Yes.

Interviewer: Yes. Your illness has actually given you an extra ability.

Eric: Yes, I can sense what is going to happen using my illness. I'm actually able to predict based on experience, what people are going to do and I can read people better now than I could before. I'm not only learning about people all the time, but I'm also adapting to changes.

Interviewer: Ok. That makes sense.

Eric: Yes.

Interviewer: What about your sister? How has your relationship with your sister changed?

Eric: She basically avoided the house at all times.

Interviewer: Wow.

Eric: Unless if she was looking after me not to commit suicide.

Interviewer: Well she kind of went off on her own as she was dealing with the situation.

Eric: She did her own thing. She actually did a presentation it Grade 11 or 12, and she said, " Yeah, my brother has schizophrenia. He just got out of the hospital." She told everyone in her class and she blew them away. I don't know if she cried.

Interviewer: Are you close to your sister?

Eric: Yes.

Interviewer: So your sister was sad. Or you're thinking she was sad.

Eric: Yes, but I won't ever ask her if she was crying when she told her classmates.

Interviewer: It sounds like it makes you sad thinking that she may have been sad. That she may have cried.

Eric: I left everything when I went into the hospital.

Interviewer: So your sister and you? How has your relationship been since the episode?

Eric: It's better now.

Interviewer: Good.

Eric: Yes.

Interviewer: That's good.

Eric: We have good times. We went sailing with one of my Mom's friends from the opera. That was fun.

Interviewer: Why do you want people to know your story Eric?

Eric: I think it would help the health care community. I think a lot of people would like to know what it's like inside someone who has schizophrenia.

Interviewer: Do you think you're schizophrenic or do you think you are Eric with an illness? Or do you think are Eric with a special gift? How do you think about yourself and schizophrenia?

Eric: I think schizophrenia is the name of the disease and I'm just Eric.

Interviewer: Is the disease a part of you or is it separate?

Interviewer: Where do you see it belongs?

Eric: It's in me. It's literally in my brain. There's nothing I can do other than just be myself. That's about it.

Interviewer: So you'd like the health care community to know a little about schizophrenia?

Eric: And to other people with a mental illness, if they write some stuff that they remember at the time or after the time of their episode. I think it really, really helps to get it out of your mind so you're not thinking about it anymore. And so you are sending a letter to God and it'll go to Him. God will handle it on the piece of paper and wherever that piece of paper goes, you will never have to think about it again. And then your mind will be that much freer. And your mind will clear.

Interviewer: Who do you think you'd like to be in 5 years? What does your life look like in 5 years?

Eric: I'd like to be in a Marketing position. Right now I want to work for Manitoba Hydro and be a part of the Marketing team there.

Interviewer: Sounds about right?

Eric: Yes, but first I have to get in and hopefully I can.

Interviewer: Do you want a family? Do you want to get married?

Eric: Yes. I want to marry the love of my life.

Interviewer: Sounds like a good plan.

Eric: Yes and have kids in the future.

Interviewer: Ok.

Eric: Yes. Essentially have a family like my parents did. And I want a dog like Mallory. I miss my dog. She died at Christmas time in 2004.

Interviewer: I see.

Eric: Yes.

Interviewer: Can you think of anything else you want to add at this point? We've sort of gone through our list of questions. Gone all around the world and back and then some.

Eric: Yes. Let's see. Well I have a friend who's doing the artwork for the hallucinations and delusions.

Interviewer: Tell me one of the most bizarre hallucinations you ever had. Did you ever hear voices or did you just see things?

Eric: Well I remember even after the whole episode at one point I was lying in bed and my back was to the door. I heard this breathing and I quickly turned to see who was there and there was no one. I was so scared that I turned on the light and went upstairs and I woke up my parents. Then I laid on the couch and I was thinking oh man it was so real. I couldn't believe it. And I thought the meds were supposed to get rid of this. But I know now that some hallucinations would appear and that the meds couldn't get all of it because it's imperfect.

Interviewer: Some day maybe.

Eric: But in a way it's kind of good that I still have a little bits of it because it reminds me. It's still there and reminds me of my Uncle who had schizophrenia. I remember he was on the bus with me while I was going home. I thought why is he on the bus with me, but I didn't approach him because I didn't know him that well. And I think he wasn't taking his meds at the time so I was kind of scared. But these kids were kind of bugging me. They were kind of my friends and they were just bugging me. My Uncle Dennis, (he liked to spell his name Denys), said to them, " Do that again and I'll boot your ass."

Interviewer: You had an ally.

Eric: And that day I told my parents that my Uncle Denys was on the bus.

Interviewer: Your Uncle had schizophrenia?

Eric: Yes, but he had it really bad. He predicted that we would be Americanized fairly quickly, or in a matter of time. But I wish my parents would share some of his thoughts of what he thought of the future would be because he was a very smart man. And with the disease he had crazier hallucinations and delusions than I did. But he was a good guy. He looked somewhat like my Dad and Uncle Bert, only taller and heavier. Uncle Denys died in October 2000. I think that it's important that I write this book for him so that his mind will be free too.

Interviewer: Sounds good.

Eric: Some of the other information?

Interviewer: Delusions that you wanted to share and some other thoughts?

Eric: Delusions. One of them is that I started thinking is God, or the Devil or Jesus are the same person/being or why are they telling me something that terrifies me that I don't want to know.

Eric: At one point I got a high. I thought I was God the Almighty and I could think things away or I could recreate. I could do whatever I wanted. And then I started thinking a normal thought. No, why am I thinking this. And then I had a feeling what if I'm like Jesus. I can't do as much but I could still have great powers. And then I hit a low, I thought, "Oh, maybe I'm the Devil." I'm bad or I can do evil things. But it was all 3 different levels all in one shot. It's really bizarre but my head hurt when I got the high. It was like something popped out of my head. It was like I was at one point I could feel connected to God and that's why I felt that way. It was just amazing!

Interviewer: Imagine there are people who never ever experienced anything like that their entire life.

Interviewer: You know, I've never.

Eric: I've never met another person with schizophrenia that's felt that. But it's such a high...everything in my mind is lit up like fireworks of ideas and thoughts. I feel like I can fly or I'm invincible. It's almost better than a high because it's natural. Well not natural, but you know the illness just makes a natural chemical that gets you that high that it's like "Wow." But to some degree some of my senses have dulled. The feelings throughout my body they're slowly coming back, but I don't think I'll ever feel the same way as I did before I was on the medication.

Interviewer: You have a good relationship with your psychiatrist?

Eric: Oh yes.

Interviewer: You mentioned that earlier too.

Eric: Yes. He and I talk about everything. He's like my priest.

Interviewer: Confession.

Eric: Yes, yes. We get along really well.

Interviewer: Good.

Eric: It helps. My next appointment seems to be every time I get stressed. So it's at the perfect time I have to see him. I tell him everything and then everything is fixed.

After that I don't know if it's because God heard me or he heard me but everything goes away. Everything calms down after I talk to him. I guess I have sorted things out with him. And being in love is different. It affects my paranoia. Which kind of sucks that love affects it. But, luckily I've got a good girlfriend and she understands somewhat. But I think she has to learn more about the disease. I don't know if she's learned about it on her own, but I think she should talk to my parents and my sister just so that she can have a better understanding.

Interviewer: How did you tell her that you had schizophrenia? Or did you tell her?

Eric: I just felt open to her and I told her. I felt like I had nothing to hide with her.

Interviewer: Right at the beginning.

Eric: Yeah, and I don't know, I just, I got a good feeling from her. I thought she was the best person in the world when I first met her. And her friends were good and I felt like they were very accepting people. So I knew, I felt like she was like the head honcho of them even though she wasn't, I thought she was and I liked talking to her. Yeah.

Interviewer: Interesting.

Interviewer: Has she expressed any concern about your illness?

Eric: She is very afraid of the next psychotic break if there ever is one.

Interviewer: How many pyschosis' have you had? One or?

Eric: One.

Interviewer: One.

Eric: And I'll be getting better as time passes on and the less severe the next episode.

Interviewer: How long has it been? Been a few years?

Eric: It's been 5 years or, well, 6 but from 1999 to 2000. My Psychiatrist said I was back to normal in November or December of 2000. He told me that he read somewhere that in 5 years from now if nothing happens, or after that, I should be good to go and not have another one or at least you will have a less severe psychosis.

Interviewer: Statistically speaking you're not as likely to have a psychotic break.

Eric: Yes. I should be ok.

Interviewer: Does this mean you can go off your medication?

Eric: Probably not, although that would be my ultimate dream. That's why I'm trying to have enough stress but not too much where it'll cause another episode. For example, if I'm too busy I will not add any more work if it can be done until tomorrow or I will delegate or ask for help if something needs to be done today. If I can't get help or finish the work then I will inform whoever needs to know.

Interviewer: Why do you want to stop taking the medications?

Eric: It's frustrating not having the same feelings. I remember at one point in the middle or near the end of my psychosis I said to my Mom, "I want my feelings back." It's like they were ripped out of me. I could feel but it was like...and that was it. And that's all that I'd feel. Where is the high I would get or the excitement that I'd feel in my brain? Like now it's just dull. But now, I get very excited about my girlfriend. When she is about to visit or we're going to do something. I get excited and I have my feelings but they're not the same. I have my emotions but they're not the same. But I still know I can: now when I stretch I can. It's coming back and I can feel the way I used to. It feels good. It's as though you lost sensation and now it's coming back and it feels good to stretch when you feel relieved and relaxed after a good stretch. And I think that being in love helps. It makes you feel really good and it brings back your emotions.

Since the first interview five years ago, I will share what happened since 2005 and the ending would be where I am presently.

My girlfriend, of whom I've been with now for 7 years as of 2010, was looking for an apartment in November 2005. She lost her job earlier that year. She was living with her friend that she knew since kindergarten and her friend's cousin. She found a new job and moved in with her parents for about a month. Then my girlfriend's nephew informed her about an apartment that was available in the same building as her aunt. So my girlfriend and I took the apartment. At that time my parents were moving to BC. And I was working at Safeway part-time and transferred to a store closer to the apartment where we lived. I was still looking for a full time job. I went to a career symposium and got help from an employment office that said they would find me one within 90 days. It was just before the 90 days that my girlfriend found an ad in the paper. I applied for the job. It was a temporary full time position and I got it. I quit Safeway in 2006. Then I got a lead for somewhere else. I got the permanent full time job there. It was customer service. I started training for my job I felt like my head was going to explode. While I was working I was feeling dizzy quite often. I would not feel good especially when I would go up and down in the elevator. But I enjoyed the job for the fact that it taught me a lot and there were nice co-workers there.

Since I had my job for 3 months and passed the probationary period. Nancy and I applied for a pre-approved mortgage. To our surprise, we were pre-approved for a mortgage and so we started looking for a house. We finally bought a house by October 2006.

In November of 2006 Nancy checked to see if she was pregnant because she needed to know if she could drink at her company's Christmas party, unfortunately, for her she found out that she couldn't drink. However she was excited about having our baby. We didn't tell anyone until Christmas and even then we only told our immediate family.

As time went on I was realizing what was going on where I was working. Near the end of the campaign at my work there were a lot of cancellations a month before it left. As time went on it seemed like mine and everyone else's service had improved. People were signing on. It seemed like the campaign was expanding near the very end. The campaign left the call centre to a company in India near the end of March. I was laid off and the company told me to wait until they had a new position for me.

At the end of March of 2007, Nancy and I went to visit my parents in BC at the same time as my grandfather and cousin was visiting them. When we arrived in BC, my parents gave us a back road tour of the Okanagan Valley late at night. It was beautiful. The next day we woke up and went to Naramata and did some wine tasting along the way. At the hotel in Naramata, we had a light lunch topped off with hot chocolate and then continued on our wine-tasting route. Of course, Nancy had to spit out each time, which is what you are supposed to do when tasting wine. The next stop was Lang Vineyard where my grandfather who had been sitting outside admiring the view with my Mom asked where we were. She told him that we were inside tasting wine, he jumped up and said let's go. Needless to say we did wine tasting. Later on we went for special ice cream on the way to the desert. The Osoyoos Desert Centre was closed before we arrived. I took Nancy to a restaurant at the shore of the lake and we had an exquisite supper. And the water was calm and the sun was setting and you could see the lights of the houses across the shore on the mountainside. Lastly, we went to Lost Moose where the elevation was 3000 feet above sea level and we had dinner watching the sunset in the mountains and had a picture taken with a giant stuffed moose.

No more than a week later, I came back from BC and was put on a new campaign at the call centre. It seemed a lot better. As time went on things were stressing me out at work. I enjoyed getting scared by my baby whenever she kicked my wife's stomach while she was pregnant. We were excited with our pregnancy. On Monday July 23, Nancy started contractions, and she did not tell me only that her parents were picking me up after work. They had been to the hospital earlier that afternoon. I worked an 8-hour shift not knowing she was having contractions. On Tuesday, she called me at work to say she was picking me up to see the Doctor. When we saw the Doctor we weren't admitted to the delivery room. The contractions weren't close enough

We stayed at the hospital Tuesday night because we told the Doctor we had no air conditioning. But by Tuesday at 5 am a Nurse told us to leave because Nancy was not far enough along. They needed the bed for someone else that was ready to deliver. So we went home to no air conditioning. We sweltered from 5 am until 3 or 4 pm. I called my mom after lunch that day. Then my Mom's friend called and asked if we wanted to spend the night at her house with air conditioning to make sure that Nancy and the baby did not get dehydrated. So we went to my Mom's friend's place until 10pm. At about 10:15 pm we arrived at the hospital. At 10:20 pm the nurse waited to see if Nancy would dilate enough. At 2 am we were officially admitted into the delivery room. Since 2 am Tuesday morning she was waiting to have our baby. By 4 pm Wednesday the baby hadn't dropped enough yet, and the baby's heartbeat had significantly dropped, so we had to have a C-section. We had a healthy baby and I cut the umbilical cord. Before the baby was born we had ultrasound pictures taken that did not reveal the gender. So it was a nice surprise when we had our daughter, Rebecca Lynn in July 2007. I was able to be with Nancy throughout her labour of 60 hours and subsequent delivery at the hospital.

Nancy's Mom stayed with us for the first couple of days. She was a great help while we rested for a few days.

The reason I was talking about Rebecca Lynn being born was because I had no symptoms of my disease showing at the time.

Prior to Rebecca being born my former psychiatrist semi-retired in the spring of 2007 and informed me that he could recommend me to a fellow psychiatrist or I could get my doctor to recommend one to me. So I saw my doctor who led me to believe that I just needed to see her for the prescriptions, since everything seemed fine at the time. Time passed and in July 2007 a few weeks before Rebecca was born I asked my doctor if she could find a psychiatrist for me. She said she would look for one. Later on I asked again. This time it was in November 2007 and my doctor did nothing. I found out that my Mom called the receptionist, of my former psychiatrist, who remembered her and booked the appointment.

I saw my former psychiatrist in November 2007 and I asked him to change my meds and he did. I felt the ones I was on were no longer working because I was not really sleeping at night and during the day I was showing signs of a psychosis. Then in January of 2008 my symptoms showed up and I had extreme anxiety. I could not breathe and I was dizzy and gaining weight. By the time February came around I had enough. I was exhausted and went to the ER with my Mom. I saw a psychiatrist. She gave me a choice; I could be admitted or put in the outpatient program. I chose to be in the outpatient program. The psychiatrist gave me about two weeks off work to start healing. Then I went back to work. I was not as bad as before. I shortened my hours with work. I had changed to short-term disability. I was accepted at the McEwen Psychiatric Ward outpatient program. While I was sick I felt like I was being pushed forward and I could not keep up. It seemed like I was out of breath when I got stressed. At some points I did not feel like I was getting any oxygen to my brain. That happened in February until mid July 2008. After all that I finally decided to change back to my old meds. When I placed my prescription the pharmacist told me that the N-risperidone had been recalled because some were not working. The risperidone was not working for me. Their pharmacy had decided to go with another manufacturer of risperidone. It was this product that I was now being given at the time my prescription was filled. It worked and risperidone continues to work on a low dose.

In the spring of 2008 the week of May long weekend, Nancy saw the sign for boot camp and wanted me to call and get in. She needed me to have more energy than I did. From my point of view I was trying very hard to help her with cleaning the house and taking care of Rebecca.

So I went to boot camp to reduce my anxiety levels. I did that for about 8 weeks 3 times a week for an hour and a half. Then I did it again in the fall for another 8 weeks. I feel it saved my life. I am very grateful for the change because now I have a lot more energy and I am participating in my family life and lost 10 pounds and my cholesterol is 5.1 which is .1 above normal. I lost inches on my waist as well.

Now I don't get dizzy when I eat or drink certain foods, whereas before I would get dizzy. A lot of symptoms went away once I started exercising. Not only that but I have more energy and I eat healthier by eating at home and only going out to eat once a week.

In January of 2009 I was reading a pamphlet that was given to me at my door and there was an excerpt from the Bible and it continued from when I read about the evil one is almost dead, I assumed it was talking about the devil when I read that in 1999, instead it finished it in another sentence stating that it was talking about Jesus being the evil one. Why I saw that or read it that way because of schizophrenia I don't know. One thing for sure there is a fight between good and evil. Just thinking about it let alone talking about it, is terrifying. What I don't understand is why and who is narrating in the bible, one of God's 'writers' who turned to the dark side? Who knows, and what do they gain from it. One thing I do know is that we as humans are being allowed to succeed and prosper by what we say or do. I know that because it says it in the Psalms and another part of the Bible.

On December 19, 2008 my Grandfather or as I called him Pepere passed away which was really sad. Fortunately, my daughter had her picture taken with my Pepere, Memere or as I called her Grandmaman (French so the 'n' is silent), my parents and Nancy. After that picture my daughter was sitting on the table facing her Great Pepere (Great Grandfather) giving each other Eskimo kisses with their foreheads touching. So we took a picture of that. We still have it.

I started documenting my anxiety a month after I stopped taking olanzapine of which I tried from November 2007 to July of 2008 and started taking risperidone my previously prescribed drug. These were the symptoms still remaining from olanzapine. Keep in mind I was attending boot camp until the end of October. The following is a record from my diary: August - October 2008

August 9, 2008: Between 8 pm and 9:30 pm I felt anxiety, dizzy, nauseas, short of breath and light headed. During that day I dug out our garden all afternoon. I had pasta for supper. I sat down outside even though I was anxious.

August 10: Before lunch I had a hard time breathing and my chest tightened. I went out for supper anyways. I find that when I'm sitting at a booth or a chair in a restaurant or at home I feel like I am falling backwards or that I'm just going to fall. When I sit back the feeling goes away and when it comes back I do the same thing.

Saturday, August 16: I went to my wife's cousin's wedding without carrying extra medication and challenged the 'crazy' thoughts, especially a déjà vu making think/believe or wonder if it's going to be the last point in my life.

Sunday, August 17: While I was sleeping my chest kept getting heavy and I was having a hard time breathing in my sleep.

Monday, August 18: Apparently I was totally fine. Nothing happened, not even a 'crazy' thought.

Tuesday, August 19: When I take a nap in the afternoon, felt pain in my left arm especially if I haven't eaten.

Wednesday August 20: Chest hurts with head propped up lying down.

5:45-5:55 pm I got into my wife's vehicle with air conditioning on, I had trouble breathing, chest was heavy, sat up, it helped a little bit, but then I had trouble breathing again. Adrenaline kicked in and my heart was beating fast.

Thursday, August 21: Woke up from nap feeling chest pain and it was as if my heart were up in my shoulders. I felt chest pain while napping at 11:30 am. I ate at 2 pm. Between 4:30 pm and 5 pm my chest felt like it was compressed and it was hard to breathe.

Friday, August 22: I was still feeling chest discomfort when I lie down. Still feels like my chest is in my shoulders again. I ate at Noon. At 3:20 pm – 4 pm I lay down and have the same effect. I thought of going to boot camp and I was excited. My chest tightened at that moment.

Sunday, August 24: I had cereal for breakfast at 1 pm. At approximately, 2:30 pm I had lunch. Soon after I bent down to look at Rebecca's foot and stood up and started wheezing, feeling dizzy, and my chest was heavy.

Monday, August 25: At 1:30 pm my ribs were sore. My chest felt heavy after having KFC/A&W chicken and strawberry milk. When I lie down and then stand up my blood feels thick and my arteries and veins hurt. 3:50 pm I had the same feeling as last week Monday. My chest feels like its in my shoulders and I feel pain while I nap.

Good news: As of last week I can shower in the afternoon without feeling chest pain or other symptoms of anxiety. I can go up and down stairs without chest changing pressure since I've been on risperidone for a couple of months.

6:50 pm: While eating supper, my chest had discomfort when I leaned forward. When I leaned back the compression/discomfort went away. How can I get rid of it while leaning forward while standing up or lying down?

Tuesday, August 26: Started eating more vegetables/ at least V8. After leaving the my appointment with the outpatient nurse at McEwen I walked downtown even though I felt chest pain, shoulder pain, I had difficulty breathing, however it was not as bad as last time. I was able to walk a straight line rather than walking at an angle to the right a little bit. Once I got off the bus I didn't vibrate as much as last time.

I've determined that since I'm getting better I must have schizophrenia as my only disease that likes to play tricks. However that doesn't mean I won't verify it physically through blood, urinalysis, ultrasound, CT tests just to make sure. The problem is how do I know when it's a true physical problem. At least colds I can figure out or infections.

Wednesday, August 27: Same chest discomfort. 7:45 pm-8:05 pm I had a panic attack on the way to picking up a video game and then to Wal-Mart. Luckily, I took my pill

5 minutes before that. It's consistent that whenever the sunsets, I have panic attacks, big, small, or none at all.

Thursday, August 28: I woke up with so much gas in my stomach that it was painful and difficult to get rid of. Coughed up mucus in the morning. At 4:10 am I had chest discomfort. I ate at 11:30 am before my nap. I didn't fall asleep until 12:30 pm and slept until 2:10 pm. At 1:44 pm I woke up my briefly because my left arm was numb. I moved it and circulation came back. I checked my arm and there were bed marks on it indicating that I had slept on it too hard. I fell asleep soon after until 2:10 pm.

Good news my nausea is gone. When I get off the bus I don't have weakness in my legs nor do I feel any vibrations at all.

Side note: My stool was black in April while I was on olanzipine while I was visiting my parents in Ste. Rose.

Friday, August 29: I was fine.

Saturday, August 30: At the Fraser family reunion there were more than a 100 people. I had difficulty breathing, especially if I went into the basement and then outside and vice versa. I had tightness in my chest and difficulty breathing just as we were leaving the family reunion to go home. Note: I had not peed for 8 hours. It was hot and humid outside. It felt like blood was flowing up but were swollen and pressure was on my chest which made it difficult to breathe.

Sunday, August 31: My left arm was sore.

September, 1: Uncomfortable to take a deep breath, because it feels like I'm pushing my heart up so when it pumps it feels squashed and it's difficult to breathe. It hurts to exhale.

September 2: I felt little to no discomfort.

September 3: I keep thinking that I'm going to die or am I going to die because I feel like crap. I got rid of the thought by telling myself it's wasting my time and I'm going to ignore until the thought goes away and by actually enjoying the time and moments with my daughter. Note:I guess we all wonder that thought, unfortunately, it happens when we're depressed or just feel like crap. To get rid of it, enjoy and be happy with what you have and everything you want will come to you. A friend told me, if you think life is tough then it's tough, if you think life is easy then it's easy. As Pepere said to me before I found my first full-time job he said, " Keep going." He told me that around Easter, I remember because I gave him and my grandmaman an Easter card in 2006.

The good thing about the brain is that if you ignore the thought that keeps reoccurring it will go away because you're not using those neurons plus you're not giving them a chance to connect to other neurons to keep associating them with good or other neurons. If you ignore neurons that have the symptoms they will disappear.

Side note: I still feel pain at the edge of my hips and left lower back at my hip bone, it feels like I'm kicked in the groin, especially on hot and humid days whether I feel good or bad mentally.

Cancel the thought that I'm going to die soon every time I have a panic attack even though it feels like it. I seem to have the thought when I'm sitting down at a restaurant or on the toilet and I have to lean forward or backwards because I lose my balance on the left side.

September 3: Same day. I had chest discomfort and I hadn't gone to the bathroom for a while today. Once I belched I felt better

September 5: Same thing.

September 6: Same thing, except I went to the washroom and was relieved.

September 7: Still hurts to take a deep breath. Good news: Because I've been inhaling and exhaling my sides of my chest loosened up. Now the front of my chest still hurts. I've concluded that sharp pain in my left abdomen is severe gas pain or caused by my anxiety. Especially when I have sweets with high sugar content or even soda.

September 8: Still same chest discomfort, even if I release gas it temporarily relieves discomfort. The same happens when I'm eating or going to the bathroom. I had a panic attack when I was driving.

September 9: Same chest pain occurs at random times.

September 10: I had chest pain on the way in the car while my wife's parents were driving me to McEwen, but it went away in a few minutes. It happened again just before catching the bus to go home. Ate an All-Bran bar and sat down, and the chest pain went away.

Living with Shadows

Good news: While I was downtown I was fine and barely felt any vibrations transferring from one bus to another going home. I'm making slow progress for getting better. I make myself aware of a situation on the bus and prepare myself as to what I am going to do to reduce my anxiety depending on the situation.

September 11: Same chest discomfort when eating or going to the washroom.

September 12: Same as yesterday.

September 13: I ate at 7 pm Saturday.

September 14: I woke up at 8 am. I went back to sleep and my veins went far below my skin and it hurt until 11:30 am, I ate cereal and the pain went to a minimum. But my chest still hurt with my head propped up while lying next to my family.

September 15: I had supper yesterday at 6:30 pm; I woke up at 6: 45 am and went back to bed at 7:30 am. Blood pressure felt low and I had difficulty breathing again. So far eating breakfast eases my breathing.

Good news: Panic attacks are at a minimum since September 12.

September 18: Chest pain started at 4 pm and continued on… I'm starting to track eating habits and patterns while I'm taking boot camp.

September 19: Chest pain started at 5 pm and continued after supper.

September 20: 6:25 pm I started wheezing before eating Chinese food. I ate Wendy's for lunch at 1:30 pm. My arteries were sore. (Duh.)

September 21: I woke up with pain in my left arm all the way into my index, pinkie fingers. I had the same pain at 3:30 pm – 4:30 pm during and after my nap except I also felt pain in my left shoulder.

September 22: My left arm was tingling again. Before I went to bed my chest was red...I'm going to check if it happens after I've done boot camp. My chest turned red once before however, I did not make a note as to what I had done prior, during or after it happened. I'm going to monitor it. I had an anxiety attack while driving from Watt St. to boot camp. My chest was not red after the anxiety attack.

September 23: I woke up this morning and it was difficult to breathe. It happens every time I wake up. Difficulty breathing was not as bad this time. I ate before bed and once I woke up. The tingling in my left arm didn't happen today.

September 24: Same thing with trouble breathing except it happened while I was sleeping. Woke up with circulation cut off to my head – it was numb. Same chest discomfort with head propped up while lying down. I eat breakfast at 7:15 am every morning. Numbness in left arm has not occurred since eating at 7: 15 am.
When it's hot and humid I have difficulty breathing especially if I have a shower the same day ... monitoring it... I asked what affects blood pressure? Caffeine, smoking, sugar and stress.

Living with Shadows

September 25: Last night my chest was tight after supper and while exercising at boot camp. My muscles were still tight this morning but not as bad as last night. I took a bath and it relaxed my muscles and I feel free... I don't feel chest pain... muscle in chest is sore as opposed to both being tight and sore. I wonder if it's indigestion that I feel because when I release gas I feel better.

September 25: This morning my hand and arm was tingling a bit. Tomorrow I will check my blood pressure in my chest. I can distract myself easier than before.

September 26: I felt pain in my left arm. I was at a football at the city's stadium game at the stadium. My chest was red in the centre once I came home... still tracking...

September 27: I went grocery shopping with my family and Wal-Mart later in the evening and I got a little bit anxious and then my anxiety went away. I had pain in my left arm.

September 28: No pain in my left arm.

September 29: Very little pain in my left arm, however my pinkie nail was white instead of pink. I learned from my Doctor that if your nail is pink you have good circulation however if it's not seek your Doctor. I had difficulty breathing this morning however I felt better than before and once I had belched loudly I was a lot better and it was easier to breathe. I am eating a lot healthier than before. I had chest pain... I had lunch at 1:30 pm and I had supper at 7 pm. why I felt chest pain for hunger is normal... for me anyways.

September 30: I had chest pain before bed so I went downstairs and had a fruit and a Tylenol. I relaxed. I woke up at 12:30 am, which was half an hour after the fruit and Tylenol and I was sweating. I fell asleep at 12: 45 am.

October 2: Pain in my left arm.

October 3: I had a left pectoral muscle cramp close to the centre of my chest. Interesting when I touch it hurts my heart. I feel pain in my chest if I lay down for too long. I haven't seen my chest turn red since September 26.

October 15: I'm getting better not worse. I had pain in my left arm. While driving to boot camp I had very little anxiety, just a little tightness in my chest and I felt normal.

So that is what I went through in 2008 and the doctors did blood tests and other tests to make sure that I was normal. I was taking care of my wife and daughter during that time. I still had symptoms but they weren't interfering or controlling my life.

Now it's August 19, 2009 and I eat at home as much as I can and more importantly I learned how to eat smaller portions and choose healthy snacks between meals. When I get anxiety my stomach creates a lot of gas that makes it harder to breathe so I cancel or delete my anxious thought and distract myself and think positive simple thoughts. For example, while I'm in traffic and feel panicked I tell myself that I can park the car and get out and ask for help. Even simpler I put relaxing music on or turn it off and look around and realize that I'm just sitting here in the car waiting to move. I ask myself, am I in hurry? No. If I am, just enjoy the view or look around at what's going on versus what's not going. The point is changing your thoughts. Do something you like doing rather than focus on what's causing the anxiety.

I am volunteering while pursuing a new career or job. I'm volunteering at Concordia hospital as a Front Lobby Ambassador and Falls Prevention Ambassador. I am also a guest speaker for the Manitoba Schizophrenia Society and a guest speaker for Selkirk Mental Health Centre through the Manitoba Schizophrenia society.

Not to mention while I was feeling or having those problems I managed to go to Disney World in Orlando, Florida. I went with my wife, daughter, parents, sister and my parent's friend with her daughter. Luckily, Rebecca started to walk about a month before we left for Orlando, Florida. We went on the kid rides, and my wife went on the adult rides with my sister. We stayed for about a week and had a great time. We finished it off with going to Downtown Disney and eating at the Planet Hollywood. My sister and dad were paid a dollar each to wear the Planet Hollywood bags on their heads by the waiter. He was pretty cool. While I was in Orlando I also went to NASA Kennedy Space Centre and Sea World where we saw Shamu. Despite all of the crowds I had a great time and my anxiety was under control.

Since then I've been getting better. I always had this negative thought of "I'm going to die." Now I can live with it and know that I can go anywhere with it and nothing is going to happen because I have to live despite the negative thought and ignore it. It gives me great hope in times of hopeless thoughts. I just think of Disney World with my family and the endless possibilities while living with that negative thought. I realize that it's the disease not me. Plus when I eat healthy the symptoms are less prevalent. Just as when my stress levels are low. I lost another 10 pounds and my dizziness only appears a little bit when I'm stressed. I feel like I'm 18 again.

The point is that you can live a prosperous life despite the negativity and experience hope and most of all life itself. It matters how you want to perceive life. The good thing is that you can change it. But be careful how you perceive life or reality. The world has to go through turmoil before it can become paradise and it will take time even though it has already begun. If you seek, you shall find. I read in Rebecca's carry-around children's Bible a positive beginning of new life. Jesus said, "... Heaven is close at hand." Now here I am to help speak for those who have and live with Schizophrenia.

My goal is to teach, understand and prevent schizophrenia. This disease can be solved with a combination of supports, exercise, eating healthy and talking about it.

Printed in Great Britain
by Amazon